TALISMAN

■ ■ ■

by
Afaa M. Weaver

TIA CHUCHA PRESS
CHICAGO

ACKNOWLEDGEMENTS

To Queen Mother Abena Joan Brown, who gave me the nudge into this part of my journey.

To my mother-in-laws, Mama Cofield, Virginia Barbee, and Sallye A. Warr.

To my friends Elizabeth Alexander, Adjoa Denise Blalock, Theresa Moore, Patricia Smith, and Madeline Tiger, who were among the first readers of this manuscript and who encouraged me to publish this collection.

To Camille Billops for her sage comments from the cornucopia of her sizzling sincerity and her marvelous art.

To all the women in my extended family and to the women who have helped me appreciate the value of platonic friendship, including Kathy Anderson, Tina Barr, Jonetta Barras, Lucille Boyd, Noni Chaney, Kelli Cochran, Claire Constantikes, Toi Derricotte, Ayanna Douglass, Sheila Glenn, Lynda Hill, Cynthia Hogue, Jackie McCrae, Carolyn Micklem, Sara Micklem, Michelle Parkerson, Alice Reid, Laurie A. Schmidt, and Barbara Zarcone, and other wonderful friends I have known over the years.

To Dr. Valerie F. Sedlak, who has been my teacher, spiritual advisor, and friend in love & light for many years.

To my sistas by birth—Marva, Michele, and Marlene, who are the loves of my life, my sweethearts.

To Patrice Wilson, who waited for me.

Poems published in periodicals and anthologies: "The Robe," "Susan Heyward," "Writing Numbers," "White Shoes and Swings," "Humility" and "Skipping" in *Patterson Literary Review*. "Michele," "Sin," and "Detroit 1985" in *Beyond the Frontier*, an anthology to be published by Black Classics Press.

Printed in the United States of America

ISBN 1-882688-17-1
Library of Congress Number: 97-62551

BOOK DESIGN: Jane Brunette
FRONT COVER ART: Franco and Tessa I by Camille Billops, copyright 1990; 22" x 30", colored pencil on paper. From the collection of James W. Jackson and Gedney L. Vining.
BACK COVER PHOTO: David Hoffman

PUBLISHED BY:
TIA CHUCHA PRESS
A Project of the Guild Complex
PO Box 476969
Chicago, IL 60647

DISTRIBUTED BY:
NORTHWESTERN UNIVERSITY PRESS
Chicago Distribution Center
11030 S. Langley
Chicago, IL 60628

Funding for this project was partially provided by the National Endowment for the Arts, the Illinois Arts Council, and the Lannan Foundation. In addition, the author received a fellowship from the Pennsylvania Council on the Arts in 1994, which helped greatly in the writing of this collection.

for Francine J. Wingfield

The lamp of the body
is the eye. It follows that if your eye is clear,
your whole body will be filled with light. But if your eye
is diseased, your whole body will be darkness.
If then, the light inside you is darkened,
what darkness that will be!

Matthew 6:22-23

I don't want no heartache on my mind.

TABLE OF CONTENTS

BESSIE

...

WHITE SHOES AND SWINGS

Before my sisters and brother
came screaming out of Mama,
she used to take me to the swings.
I had white shoes from a store
that claimed to correct flat feet.
The park had trees full of wisdom,
like the full dresses of women
I watched with four year old eyes.
Swinging easily, back and forth,
I trusted Mama not to push me away
to some place where I could not
get back to her, where I would be
eaten by dark fear. She was young,
but I did not understand what it was
to be a young mother who didn't know
nothin bout raisin boys, what boys need.
I just knew I had Mama all to myself.

MARVA   My Aunt Hilda stayed with me
while Mama had my first sister.
Aunt Hilda was my devilish aunt
who liked dirty jokes and pranks,
but we just played while Mama
was singing pain, birthing Marva.
One day Mama came up the stairs
walking slow and heavy, real heavy,
with this blanket full of dark chocolate.
I peeped inside and saw a plump baby,
my first sister. After that, Christmas
was not the same. There were
two chairs at my play kitchen table.

MICHELE My baby sister used to get
her baths on the kitchen sink.
We were in our new house
in a neighborhood where white folk
used to live, but they left fast.
Everybody was colored now,
and we did colored kinds of things,
like bathing babies in the kitchen.
That's the first I remember Michele,
brown and naked up on the counter
in that little, plastic baby tub.
She had her legs up in the air,
feet kicking around, smiling.
I tiptoed on nine year old feet
and looked all over this baby sister.
I looked between her legs
for a long time, just a studying.
Her pee hole looked like a keyhole.
Mama said all girls was like that,
and I knew what boys had because
I was a boy. I had questions.
"Mama, if that is a keyhole,
what is the key? Where is the door?
What house is we in anyway?"

THE ROBE

Mama and her sisters
were dancing in the living room,
cackling, bending the floor.
I was downstairs in the tub,
scrubbing my knees with Ajax,
wondering where the black
came from, where it went.
I was afraid to cross
the living room sea of women
with their party, afraid of what
I did not know of women,
their delight in measuring
the sex of naked little boys.
They prophesied a boy's
potential to please a woman
by studying hairless pricks.
Afraid more of being late for bed
than of being seen, I put on
my yellow robe. I wrapped myself
like a fireman about to enter
a burning building, and I climbed
the stairs where my mother
stood with her mischievous smile.
I walked into this room of women
who loved me, and my mother
pulled off my robe for all to see
what kind of man I could be.
Shame cut me like a cleaver.
Once in a nightmare, I saw
my mother at the top of the stairs,
face raging, hair full like Medusa,
daring me to climb, daring me.

MT. ZION BAPTIST

Before Grandma couldn't walk,
we all went to church together sometimes.
We sat in one little group on the pew
like the pictures of black folk
on the backs of the fans we used
to cool ourselves in the church.
Mama wanted me to always do things
like they supposed to be done.
Her word for right was *businessfied*.
Even now when I am making love,
the woman gotta know I'm *businessfied*.
The singing was usually good,
and I knew all about this church.
I was in Sunday School and on
the Junior Usher Board.
I went to Baptist Training Union.
One Sunday in winter we went
to morning service, and I got bored.
I was getting to be fifteen,
feeling like a man, smelling my pee,
as Mama and her sisters called it.
So I put my hands behind my head
in church and closed my eyes.
I didn't want to hear that mess
the pastor was dragging out himself.
We went home and Mama told me
to go in the back room and take
my clothes off and get ready for a beating.
I took off everything except my underwear
and waited for her. She came in
like the roll of thunder and beat me.
I cried the cry of shame. I wanted Daddy
to come and save me. Mama had
gone stone crazy on my behind.
When she knew she was dying,
Mama apologized to me.
It was spring. I was thirty years old.

WRITING NUMBERS

She decided to go in business,
get herself some paper and pencils,
talk on the phone all morning.
Everything was figures,
dreams, sales receipts, voices
from the television and radio,
radio preachers with secret codes.
On Friday evenings, Mister Joe
would come, this scroungy-looking
white man with a bulge in his jacket.
Mama would give him papers
and some money. She got to keep
some of it. Aunt Peaches was in business
right along with Mama, both of them
talking about three digit numbers.
Once, Aunt Peaches had to go to jail
to speak on this business of hers
and Mama's, and Mama panicked.
She wrapped up all her numbers
in little bits of aluminum foil
and froze them in the freezer.
Them numbers couldn't go nowhere.
They was stuck in ice and couldn't
combinate themselves or repeat or nothing.
She didn't stay in business
with numbers after this. She did hair.
Later on Mama told me that bulge
in Mister Joe's jacket was a gun.

VARICOSE VEINS

The older she got, the more lumps
she got on her legs. They just rose up
like humps on a train of camels or
the rough parts of a map that showed
where the mountains was s'posed to be.
I wondered how the blood got back
up to Mama's heart with all that
travelling over and through those lumps.
Sometimes they wasn't so big because
she wasn't so tired, I guess, and
I was always always afraid to touch
them things because I knew they
wasn't supposed to be on Mama at all.
They was like markers saying something
was wrong somewhere inside.
I didn't like to touch the bumpy
parts of maps neither, even
if they was s'posed to be mountains,
like they really part of the earth.

HERSHEY'S CHOCOLATE

Some nights
she would make
herself a pan of pure
chocolate. By herself
she would dip it out
with a spoon and
eat it like it was
a dessert from some
fine restaurant.
She did it so she could
enjoy herself, she said.
But when I watched her,
something in her
made me want
to cry. I knew Mama
wasn't just enjoying herself.
She was forgetting.
It takes growing up
to learn to forget,
but sometimes all it takes
is being a little boy.

MISS NOSY

She was always signifying,
poking around in somebody's business.
Mama was the news bureau
of the whole damn neighborhood.
She was the village queen mother,
as all her village sisters brought bits
of business to her about themselves
and other folk, too. Mama seemed
to draw everybody's confidence.
She thought she knew everything
and could change people's lives
by listening and then answering.
Folk come to me with stories, too.
I don't talk as much as Mama,
so they have to study me a while.
Folk come to me like I'm some
resting stone or something.
When she was dying, Mama
told me one of her secrets—
Daddy was gonna get himself
another woman before she got cold.
The only some kinda woman
Daddy got is the memories that rise
every time he go to Mama's grave.
He stands there talking silent talk,
his foot half covering his name.

HOUSE TRAINING

Every Saturday morning,
I got up before everybody else,
everybody except her.
She always had one eye open.
With my bucket and my rags,
I cleaned the kitchen and
the rest of the basement, scrubbing
the yellow walls that are still
yellow after forty years.
Scraping and rubbing, I got
the black and white kitchen floor
so bright the tiles shined when
I put on the liquid wax. I had
the bathroom looking like a picture.
Mama was proud of me, and
she talked with her sisters about
how nice I did everything. I could cook.
I could wash clothes and iron, too.
One day one of Mama's sisters said,
"Michael sure will make some girl
a mighty fine husband, mighty fine."
Only God and Mama knew the truth—
Mama was preparing me to be alone.

SKIPPING

The principal
of my elementary school,
a man with crooked fingers,
called Mama and Daddy.
They came to the school
and I had no idea
of what I done wrong.
That evening they told me
I was going to a white school
that was new. I was going
to skip the eighth grade.
For the next five years,
I had four hours of studying
every night cause they
made me go to a high school
that was tough. It was Mama's
doing. After the sixth grade,
I never went to a black school,
except one semester at Morgan.
I was angry with Mama for years
for setting me up in a class
full of mostly white children.
I still remember my black teachers
from Ft. Worthington elementary,
Mr. Jones with his bald head,
Mrs. Louis who sneaked and drank,
Mrs. Miller who got murdered.
Them teachers could teach
cause they didn't wonder who we was.
In them white schools, white folk
just right away figured you was not
up on their level, wherever that was.
In high school a white teacher,
old dried up Mr. Sullivan,
told me I was a barbarian.

HUMILITY Mama knew when I was a baby
that I was arrogant, a sweet
little boy but full of pride.
A man came with a camera when
I was just three and took pictures
of me and Cousin Bonita.
I sat up with my legs crossed,
looking just like the prince I was.
I had a lot of heart, like boys
used to say about courage.
My first grade teacher said
I was a born leader, I had something
that made it easy for me to be
in control of a situation.
Mama kept telling me I had
to be humble in this life,
so I hid this power of mine
behind smiles and knew in secret
that I was the smartest boy
in the world. Some part of me
wanted to seize life, and some part
was afraid of what life would seize in me.
Mama mixed things up sometimes,
saying be humble and then be a man.
Like the time this girl tried
to beat up my sister Marva who I was
supposed to protect. I just stood
while the girl cussed my sister out,
but she didn't hurt Marva. I knew
this girl wasn't nothing but mouth.
But Mama got mad at me for not
beating this girl out there in the alley.
Mama was always mixing me up,
and I knew I had to do what she say.
So I went in my room and felt guilty
for not smacking this girl in the face.
I thought about what I should have done,

and my anger got bigger and bigger.
Mama made up her courage.
She was always mouthing off about
what she would do to somebody.
I was going to a white school then,
and I wanted to tell Mama bout herself,
bout the ways of the white man's world.
Mr. Charlie let black girls scream and cuss
all they want to, all the damn day long,
but he dares black boys to say a word,
a mumbling word, or he will kill us.

EPSTEIN'S

When she felt like shopping,
we went to Highlandtown,
where the white folk lived.
We went to Epstein's, the store
she thought was like Macy's.
Epstein's had everything—
linen, toys, furniture—and it was
in the middle of this shopping district
stores on both sides of the street.
I followed Mama around hoping
to get something but afraid to ask.
It wasn't like when I was the only child
and we went to the market together.
I always got something from
the toy rack in Mondawmin's Food Fair.
I was too old to beg for things,
but sometimes Mama would treat me.
I was her shopping buddy cause
the girls was too little to go,
much less know what they was going for.
So it was me and Mama together
in the store, just like the old days.
I just didn't feel comfortable around
all those white folk, and I paid attention
to the way they talked to her and all.
I felt better when we was driving home,
and I could see our part of town
over the bridge that crossed over
the small steel mill near our house.
I was becoming Mama's little man.

SEARS ROEBUCK

Mama used the telephone
to change her voice.
When she ordered something
from Sears, she got proper,
proper and strange sounding.
It wasn't like Mama to be so fancy
cause she wasn't that way
around us. I just knew
she was talking to a white person
cause she did the same thing
when the insurance man came.
She was like a actress,
figuring in her head this woman
she had to be for a few minutes.
I guess she did it right cause
she took care of all her business.
Except it didn't seem right to me,
to be more than one way.
Mama loved telephones, and
I grew up and found out most women
love telephones and talking.
Most men don't have much to say,
unless they just bragging and lying.
Even then black men don't change
as much as women do most times.
Daddy didn't carry on on the phone
like Mama did. Matter of fact,
he didn't have much to say noway.
He just sat around and read the paper,
but Mama would get on the line
and go through a million changes.
Still the one that bothered me most
was changing up for white folk.
I didn't understand this English,
where it came from, where it could go,
or how Mama taught me translation.

MAMA AND HER MAMA

Grandma made her think
she was a dumb little girl.
She called Mama a knotty head convulsion,
but Grandma was mean to my aunts, too.
One day Aunt Ruby did something wrong,
and Grandma threw a rock
right at her head down home in Virginia.
Aunt Ruby said she heard the rock whistling
past her ears like a missile or a bullet.
Grandma was real hard on my mama,
and Mama never got over it.
Grandma spent her last sixteen years
with us in our house on Federal Street.
After her cane, she couldn't walk,
so Mama had to serve her upstairs
where she was in her hospital bed.
We called her Big Mama like black folk
call the grandmother what's over all else.
Sometimes Big Mama was so mean to Mama
that she came downstairs and cried.
She always wanted to please her mother.
I guess Mama wanted to be the little girl
her mother would be proud of. Here she
was doing her best to keep Grandma pretty,
with ribbons on her hair and flowery gowns.
Big Mama and Grandpa was full
of North Carolina Indian blood. Dr. Adams,
a black man with a yacht, said we
had cheekbones and hair from Cherokees.
I always wanted to be Geronimo, Cochise,
or Crazy Horse when I was a little boy.
My heart would make Mama see hers.
We would come riding on ponies
to Big Mama standing, patting her foot.
Mama would hop off, walk over real slow,
touch her mama and get the love

what made her sit and cry in her hands.
Grandma and Mama had choke holds
on each other. They spinned together
right out of this world, one after the other.

THE BRA

Mama was kinda big,
and I was her little helper
cause I was big and strong.
When she was getting ready
to go out somewhere,
she called me to help her
get herself into this bra of hers.
She would tussle with her titties
and get them in the cups,
and she would call me to hook
those clasps on the back.
Sometimes the strings inside
my fingers would squeak while
I strained to pull things together.
Mama would move around
and hold herself to get smaller
until we got her titties under control.
She called them her jugjugs.
When I was starting to feel
like a man, she would tease me,
"Come get some jugjug. "
"Come here Sugar, come here, Baby."
The first time a girl got naked
with me I unhooked her bra in back,
and her titties jumped out real full.
I felt like I was in Wonder Land. I
knew I was hooked on jugjug,
and I was sure nough Sugar . . . Baby.

PEEPING TOMS

Cousin Geff talked me into
peeping under the bathroom door
at this woman taking a piss.
We was in my Aunt Ruth's house.
Might have been something different
if we was in some strange place
where we could have escaped.
But we broke the law in jail.
Down on our little knees,
we thought we was being real sneaky,
and we tried to see up this lady's dress.
She heard us and went upstairs
and told Aunt Ruth and our mamas.
We got the ass whoopings
of our lives, with belts from our mamas.
Next time I saw cousin Geff,
I was mad with that boy because
I was supposed to see something
that I had never seen before.
All I saw was darkness,
with shadows whispering real tight
voices like when mama was tired
and had to take off them trifling
stockings clipped on that mean girdle.
She said "Whew! Lord, Jesus!"

PERMISSION

Grandma was sitting out back
with her crochet needle,
hooking in and out, making lace.
My friend Cedric was chasing
Cousin Bonita in the alley,
talking about *pussy*, talking loud.
Grandma just played like
she ain't heard nothing,
going on hooking in and out.
Cedric was running Bonita
around on the grassy hill
where you could stand and see
the cemetery that was like the sea.
I was getting nervous cause
my mama's mama was as slick
as her daughter. That's why
they was always fussing, two of a kind.
I was just hoping and praying
that Grandma would let this slide
cause I wasn't in this mess.
I was inside the fence watching,
but Grandma told Mama,
and I got a beating for saying *pussy*.
My fascination with pussy got put
on hold for a while until it was cool
with Grandma and Mama.
They knew they punished me
for something they hoped I would get
a whole lot of anyway someday,
and I knew they was laughing at me.

BLESSING OF A MAN

Uncle Geth always
bragged about how much
man he was. He had macho
from down in North Carolina
where it's like corn liquor,
strong enough to kill.
He used to stand on
one leg and sort of wiggle
the other, holding a cigarette.
When they was young
and courting the Davis girls,
both him and Daddy
had a liking for Mama.
One day Mama figured
she was gonna fix Uncle Geth
with his bragging about
his manhood. She went to work
with some boxer shorts,
a sock, and a needle and thread.
She stuffed the sock,
a great big old sock she found.
When it was finished,
Uncle Geth came over one Sunday,
as my family convened in
my house on the holy day.
Mama went in the bedroom
and pulled out the boxer shorts.
"Since you so much a man,
tell me if you can match this! "
Mama popped this giant dick
from out of the underwear,
and Uncle Geth and everybody
laughed so hard they was making
noise all in the neighborhood.
Mama made a king size johnson.

Years later a girlfriend
trapped me in her vestibule.
She was angry with me and wanted
to make me angry. She told me
bout how she loved this ten inches
a man socked to her a few times.
I remembered Mama's experiment.

If I had had the pipe to be beat,
I coulda sent this girl to the heaven
where she wanted to go.
I still had a prime lesson to learn.
The key ain't how thick and long it is.
It's how long it can last.

BESSIE   The way I heard it
Mama and Daddy was both
working at the steel mill.
Mama was in the lunch room,
and Daddy was in the mills
what looked like a smoke town.
It wasn't like they just had met
cause down home in Virginia
the Weavers and the Davises
was real tight families
the way black folk used to be.
So Mama had been knowing
this big, skinny man from
her own home who was quiet
but real mean-looking. People
say the Weavers got their evil streak
from the Webb part of the family.
Great Grandma Webb used
to kick at children and cats
when she was a old blind woman.
Anyway Mama and Daddy
wasn't no strangers at all.
Mama liked to dance and kiss
and laugh and talk. She liked
to play practical jokes.
She kept something going on.
Mama put sunshine and wind in
the wish and sigh that Daddy was.
It was right after World War II.
Daddy looked like a gangster
in his suit and tie, and Mama
looked like his partner, his running buddy.
I never heard him call her *Elsie Lee*.
She charmed him to call her *Bessie.*

MAMA'S HOODLUM

The summer
out of high school
I started drinking and
hanging out with tough boys.
I carried a knife cause
we didn't bother much
with guns. The older, tougher
men had Roscoes of
various calibers. I drank
Thunderbird and Pineapple Richard's
cause they was less than
a dollar for a whole fifth.
The next day your head felt
like it was slapped against
the Grand Canyon. We raced
my father's car and almost
killed ourselves quite a few times.
We threatened people
and was generally thought
to be a gang. We was Big Time
in Baltimore. Some of my boys
shot up heroin and smoked reefer.
One night I got so high
my friends dumped me on my porch.
Mama opened the door,
and I fell into the living room,
rolling around like a seal.
I was wrestling with my manhood.
Mama went for my wallet,
and I stood up as if to hit her.
Daddy jumped up like Joe Louis,
and I was bout to cry but I broke
for the back door and disappeared.
Daddy tried to follow me
in his car I used for racing,
but I hid in a friend's house.

Then I jumped in a cab and
went to Danny's house, where
I slept. Danny's father was
the president of Coppin State College.
Cousin Geff brought me home
the next day after I called
from Uncle Geth's to apologize.
There was nothing like being high,
feeling brave, having the respect
of other boys who swore to die for me.
"Mike, man, I would go down for you."
Music like *Junior Walker and the All-Stars*
playing "I'm a roadrunner, Baby.
Can't stay in one place too long,"
while I raced city streets at seventy
miles per hour in summer time.
Being bad felt so good and right
while Mama sat home and worried
about how and when I might die.

COMMON SENSE

Mama said I ain't had none.
I spent so much time studying
books that I didn't know
nothing about the ways of people,
especially women. She was
the only woman I knew well
and she was always busy with
the housework and minding us.
Her sisters kept her on the phone.
She had to keep them straight.
Aunt Ruth was too easy to cry.
Aunt Grace was just plain crazy.
Aunt Hilda was always borrowing
five dollars that she didn't pay back.
Mama had a full life with all this mess,
and she was so pretty in her pictures.
She was brown-skinned, a little lighter
than me. I'm more brown than red.
The first girl I loved reminded me
of Mama, but she was not as good.

SUSAN HEYWARD

The television was my friend.
Susan Heyward reminded me
of Mama cause Mama was small one time,
and Susan sounded like Mama sounded
when she was talking to white folk.
She had the same smile Mama had,
and I thought she was real pretty in a way
I wouldn't dare think about Mama.
Lord, I thought Susan Heyward was sexy,
me with my funny-looking self with bumps
and them ugly eyeglasses I had to have.
If I had really been thinking, I would have
thought Susan Heyward might have figured
Mama to be a "nigger woman" and me
to be a ugly little nigger boy.
I would have smashed that television
and watched the lies about beauty break
on the floor like phony old diamonds.
I would have listened to the radio,
except there was some things on there
Mama wouldn't let me listen to at all, like
Elijah Muhammad and the Black Muslims.
Mama said Elijah was saying things
that was just plain evil—like how to hate.

MARK AND MARLENE

It was embarrassing
to tell the boys
in the dormitory
my mama was pregnant.
I was trying to get
my first shot of leg in life,
and here you was knocked up.
So I kept quiet,
but I was proud to know
another one of us was coming,
even though I was old enough
to be the baby's father.
We argued cause I was feeling
like a man and you still wanted
to tell me what to do.
"Cut that Afro mess off
before you visit me in the hospital."
When the baby came,
it was two babies, my only brother
and my third sister. You cried.
They were hard ones, with a Caesarean.
Daddy was in there with you,
walking around in your blood,
as you hollered, "Tie the tubes!"
You was thirty-nine, old to me.
I thought you and Daddy knew
more about not getting pregnant.
A year later I knocked up a girl.
I found out what a joy it can be
to think you let one slip by.
I shoulda been afraid to
pluck a baby from the tree
that is heavy with them in heaven.

KILLING WITHOUT A KNIFE

I always fell in love with women
who could not fall in love with me.
Mama said I was a sucker
for pretty women and they used me.
One pretty woman fell for me,
after I kept trying and trying
with all them nasty bumps on my face.
We was just eighteen and didn't know
what all it took to have a house,
or how old folk had quiet time together.
I got this pretty girl pregnant.
I dropped out of the university.
We wanted to be married and live
with Mama and Daddy upstairs.
Mama asked me why I didn't use
no rubbers with this girl, and I said
I didn't take showers with raincoats.
Mama told me this would follow me
all my life, this marriage, this child.
I laughed at her and she cried a hurt
so deep I could not feel it.
Sitting on the stairs tasting tears,
she looked at me pulling away and said,
"You don't need no knife to kill. "

THE INCOMPLETE HEART

When my son was born retarded,
Mama forgot she had begged me
to get an abortion and send this boy
back to God. He had Down's Syndrome,
complete with a heart that was without
a wall between the lower chambers.
His blood ran through his body
without proper direction, like love.
One morning he did not wake up,
after the daily rushes to the hospital,
after ten months of trying to live,
of smiling when I tickled him but
not being able to sit up or develop.
I went with my wife to a department store
to buy his funeral outfit. We was just
children our damn selves, just children,
and we had to bury this first son
we had named a junior. At the funeral,
his mother tried to take him out
of the casket, and we had to pull
her back and make her sit down.
Girl, let the dead go, let him go.

I cried a little but mostly was a man,
until a year later when I drove
through the city, chased by police
at high speed from the cemetery.
I was on the television and everything.
They had me in chains, and I crawled
over to Mama and cried on her knees.
I had gone insane. I wanted to forget
the power was given to God,
who had took my son and my mind.

COLOR-STRUCK

At your funeral
we had yellow mums
around your brown casket.
I may be color-blind,
but I like yellow with brown.
You believed in your heart
I was color-struck, hooked
on light-skinned women.
You left without finishing
explaining to me secrets
of how to stop following this
path in my heart. I keep
following my heart and its aches
to where they think love is.
I sometimes do sorta lean
toward high-yellow women.
Sometimes I look at white women,
and they always lookin at me.
If I could explain something
to you, it would be that
yellow is the color of Osun.
Mama, she's an orisha.
She is what you were
because Mark & Marlene
is twins and twins run with us.
Osun always breaks my heart.
She flirts to break a man down.
Mama, all the way down.
We all carry one of these *orishas*
in our souls, our guardian spirits.
Sango of thunderbolts lives in me.
He is The General who loves
sex & hot sauce on fried chicken.
He can make Osun behave.
You could have told me this
in your way in your brown wisdom

if you had not died so young.
But I know Osun will not give me
peace until I show her Sango in me.
He mean like I am inside.
Mama, Sango's color is red.
Remember that red shirt I loved?
All along I been lookin for me.

ELEANORA

...

STOOPS, 1969

You couldn't leave
the steps cause
your stepfather Mr. Piggy
was strict as iron.
So you flirted
with me when you
got permission to go
to the store. I was
on Aunt Lois's stoop
with my cousin
and some of my boys.
I was home
from college, holding
on to home, away
from the white sea
at the university.
I hadn't made love
to a girl, and I was
feeling desperate
to keep face.
I had been in love
three times, once with
a girl from Aruba,
but I thought I could
keep you. The other girls
dropped me or never
let me in their hearts.
You loved to laugh,
and you was so pretty
you made men turn
their heads while they
was driving. I felt proud
to have a girl that could
pull any man she wanted.

SIN, 1969

It was better
than anything I had
ever done in
my whole life.
We took our clothes
off in a bedroom
in Aunt Grace's house
when the grownups
was gone. I looked
at your golden brown
skin near yellow,
and your titties full
and the thick bush
of hair on your pussy.
I was charged
like electric had
taken over my blood.
We made love
without even thinking
about making a baby.
We walked outside.
It was a sunny day.
I could feel the heat
in my chest cause
it was sticking out.
I wondered why anybody
would want this
to be a sin.

EVERYWHERE, 1969

Whenever we had
the chance, whenever
we thought nobody
was looking, we did it.
We made love in
cars, on people's sofas,
in parks in daytime
and nighttime.
We was a little
play happening every
chance it got with
only the sun, moon,
and stars for our audience.
The world was
our little enchanted
forest, and we was skipping
along, naked, holding
hands, touching our
tongues, feeling ourselves
all over, ignorant
to the fact
we was being
watched by
human eyes.

HOOKED, 1969

Any man
who loves women
understands
a junkie's needs.
With women,
you can get hooked
on sex or on love.
You can get hooked on both
and not know
the damn difference.
Back in the day,
you was my first
real love.
I don't know
how it happened.
One day
I felt like
I couldn't live
without your touch.
I couldn't live
without seeing
your body naked
near the window
at night after
we made love.
I felt I was
a man.

THE ARMY, 1970

We got married
the day after Christmas
in my mama and daddy's
living room, you
full of our first son,
full of baby.
On New Year's Eve,
I was in a cold barracks
in Ft. Leonard Wood,
on a cold mountain.
I had one blanket.
Soon they gave me
clothes, a gun,
and a new family.
I used to write to you
a whole lot cause
I missed you.
It was not easy
learning how to kill
people I didn't even
know, how to cut them
and blow holes in them.
I wrote you letters,
letters that made
you feel dumb.
I was really
the stupid
one.

SEPARATIONS, 1971

We was
always breaking up,
arguing. I
counted fourteen
separations
once when I was
counting. I missed
a few every time,
so I stopped counting.
You threw all
your stuff in a plastic
bag and went over
to your people,
Mr. Piggy and Mama Cofield.
It was downright
exasperating. We
still wanted to do things
people our age wanted
to do, and we had
this sick child.
The doctor told me
he would not live.
You did not
believe me.

HEAVEN, 1972

It was winter,
one of them times
you had left.
You was sleeping
upstairs in the house
Mr. Piggy moved
to. I was teaching
English in a high school
and working in
the Procter & Gamble
factory at night.
I got to class
early, and the office
called me over
the intercom.
I had a family
emergency at the hospital.
I drove our new car
at top speed and left
in the middle
of the street.
Mr. Piggy and
everybody else was
sitting there. You
were crying. I asked
"Where is my son?"
The doctor would not
let me see what
Death leaves behind.
Mr. Piggy said
we was paying for
our sins.

KALA, 1972

I agreed
to try to have
another baby.
The doctors said
chances were this
one would be normal.
We made love
one night with every
intention of getting
pregnant. You
even held your legs
straight up in the air
after I came to
make sure the semen
would flow to your
womb. I was still
afraid of sickness
and death in children.
You got pregnant.
I was still grieving
our dead child
we named
Junior,
Schan.

TALL SECOND SON, 1973

Kala was born,
and I was
in the hospital, too.
I had gone crazy.
The nurses
took me over
to see this giant,
chocolate baby what
was rocking them
little cradles in the room
for the newborn.
I said "Is this my boy?"
"This child look like
he already six months old."
He looked like he wanted
to talk. Years later
I got into reincarnation,
as most of the world is.
A friend told me
this soul had fought
very hard to be with me
in this lifetime.
My ancestors
had done sent me
a warrior through
the woman who
was my hard
and tough
love.

MARY, 1974

My depression
was too much for you
and me. I didn't want
to do anything.
So you fell in love
with a singer, one
of the *Softones*.
That didn't help me
in my depression, but
a woman gotta do
what she gotta do.
I just turned into a
river of my own sorrow.
I could not see
the water that I was.
I followed rumor
after rumor, tried
to catch you in the act.
I begged you at the
foot of our bed to take
me back. I had no pride.
My friend Mary
at the factory was really
a friend. She said
she would pretend to
be my woman one night
and go to the club
on Charles Street where
the *Softones* was singing.
Mary went with me,
and I felt like a sick man
with a kind and good nurse.
That was the truth,

as I had a healing.
You got jealous.
Mary was a beautiful,
chocolate brown woman.
I felt safe.

THINGS, 1974

In the apartment
that was our last home,
I wanted nice
furniture. I wanted
a home that was
a home. So we got
solid cherry pieces
for our bedroom.
It was dark and rich
and made me want to
just stand and rub it.
We had maple
in the living room
with a stereo and
a color television. It
all went back to
the store when I fell
short on the payments.
The props for this
little play of ours
were taken away
as we got in
the final act.
They were only
things.

RONETTA

...

ANNIE OAKLEY, 1974

On our first date,
we went to the movies.
I always will think
of us along with
The Godfather.
When I first took you
around my people,
you wanted to carry
your .38 in case
one of my relatives
said some reckless shit.
It was blue steel,
full of bullets and
bigger than your purse.
You became my second wife,
and I saw why you thought
you had to protect
yourself. People and God
was always taking shit
away from you and giving you
the raw deal. God
gave you diabetes. Your mama
embarrassed you, and
your stepmama didn't like
to see you darken her door.
So you smoked Salem 100s
and loved to watch
musicals more than any
kind of movie—grand colors,
love songs, and dancing,
with your loaded purse.
Where else could you go?

BROWN BAGS, 1975

It started with you
coming over on the weekends.
I would pick you up
in that car I hated.
You would have a few things
in a brown bag and spend
the weekend with me,
sitting up watching television.
We was like two bushes
that just woke up one day
and found out they was planted
next to each other.
I tried to bust the trap
we called a relationship.
You got furious and pregnant.
The doctor said your diabetes
would make the baby sick
and advised us to abort it.
We didn't want to do it.
I ended up in the hospital,
after being so depressed
I felt like I didn't wanna live.
Life had dealt us some serious
complications, and we was too young
to believe we should have
to live with struggles that could
take us out of this world
if we made a wrong turn.
So we turned into each other.
We drove head-on into
each other's pain, the things
that made us wonder if there
was any happiness anywhere.

COLUMBIA CITY, 1975

On the weekends,
we drove to places
that were soothing to see.
This was a planned city
with a gorgeous mall.
There was a lighter air
around you when we
drove away to places where
we wished we could live.
I looked at the houses
that were far too expensive,
and I dreamed, too.
At the lake, we often
walked and sat. I took
pictures of you cause I thought
I was a photographer
and a writer. I was gonna
even try making films.
I was gonna get to my dreams
with my writing. I had friends
in Washington who knew me
as being a writer. You didn't
trust them. You were gonna
get your dreams by keeping me
in the factory, where everything
threw my imagination upside
the wall like it was under arrest.

PATRICE, 1976

The poet I fell in love with
was as tall as I was and gifted
with a spirit above the mess
of most of life. We did
simple things like sit on a hill
and eat fried chicken. She
gave me a copy of poems
by Kenneth Patchen.
I first saw her at school,
the university I left for my first wife.
I had finally hooked up
with a girl that was on my
vibration level. We was in love.
She wrote me letters
that I kept for a long time.
I used to pull them out and read
them to remember what
we had. You found the letters
and burned them up. You was
mad enough to kill, so you killed
my links to an island of happiness,
and it floated away from me.

VIRGINIA, 1982

Your mama had
a nervous condition.
She used to jerk and twitch
when she was standing,
but she loved herself
some Paul Laurence Dunbar.
Every Christmas she would
recite "Christmas on the Plantation."
Herman would be
making his special dinner.
When they got that house
on the West Side, we had
a good time. Virginia
rolling into that dialect from
slavery. Herman sipping his
spirits. Your mama was in high form,
rolling up and down through
that language we still remember.
Sometimes she would
get suddenly mean and say
things we didn't expect, or she
would have this look on her face
like a question mark.
She heard all the ghosts
we had ever been.

GUNS, 1983

I made you
get rid of that .38,
but a few years later
you fought my son.
He was just a boy,
but he was big.
Your cousin Linda
came over one day
and brought a bag.
I knew you had been
talking about a gun.
I asked you
if it was a gun, and
you just smiled
a crazy smile. I felt
what only a woman
must feel for her child.
Kala was only
nine years old.
I sent him
away. I stopped
buying your
food. We went
to war.

LEAVING, 1984

Our marriage
was a bridge built
from need to need
and of need. It
was cracking up.
I waited until you went
to work one day,
and I took only what
I needed, books and clothes.
It was like being the
pink part of a wound
in the flesh while
somebody cutting it
with broken glass.
We had made
enough happy times
for me to cry while
I packed, but some
of those tears were for
the struggle I had
with myself.
Where did I go
with the time I spent
with you?

AISSATOU
...

SECOND STORY BOOKS, 1983

Baltimore was having
a literary high time.
I was one of the stars,
in the newspaper all the time,
recognized around town.
I was the black literati
of the star poets. One day
I came into the bookstore.
You was playing peekaboo
with me, Girl. Every time
I caught you looking,
you ducked down to put away
some books. We was
into a thing already, but I was
hooked up in my sadness,
looking for a way out,
not knowing the way
was inside, deeper, deeper.
I learned your name
and practiced saying it—
Aissatou Aissatou Aissatou

CORRESPONDENT, 1984

In Jamaica for six months,
you saw the revolution.
You told me how you was
an island hero when you cut
your finger with a machete
working in the fields. Bullets
was flying all around you.
You defied the middle class
and socialized with country folk
in your own house in Jamaica
away from bourgeois pretension,
playing like you was rustic like
one night I found you way
in the back of the bookstore.
You was sitting at the typewriter
with just a bra on, sweating
in big beads. Your brown skin
was just like my mother's.
Both of y'all is serious heroes.
Mama had a cut on her finger.
Her sisters cut her with a saw
in their little girl revolution
against being bored in the fields.
My mama was for real country,
with big, crusty feet, and
you would have crusty feet, too,
but you got too many table manners.
Mama didn't have many.
When she wrote her letters,
she was a chicken scratching in sand

THE HARDWARE STORE, 1985

You had so much stuff
in this apartment over
the Hardware Store that
I was afraid to light
a cigarette. In your kitchen,
I found my way to the chair
and just forgot about moving
until it was time to leave
in the early morning dark.
You lived on coffee
and cigarettes and vegetables.
We talked and talked
about everything it seemed,
but you can't talk about everything
when you getting to know somebody.
There is too much shit to tell.
Life just accumulates that way.
I looked at your art work,
the pieces that were installed
in Riverside Park in New York
and all the little things around.
One day I watched you
make a doll you later gave to me.
You put secrets in it.
A year later in a fit of anger,
I mailed it back to you.
Sometimes my own cruelty
surprises me. You never give
back a gift from any artist
to hurt them. It's worse
than killing a child.

THE BATH, 1985

In the Victorian tub
in the cold back room,
I gave you a bath.
We let the hot water
steam up the room,
and I rubbed you
with your own soap.
Your skin was wet
and dripping like
you was a honey flower
blooming from
the water. You smiled
when I dried you off.
We walked back
to the warm kitchen
thick with your things
and had coffee.
No man had ever
given you no bath,
and I had never
bathed a woman.

DETROIT, 1985

We made love
in the shower, filling
the stall with steam
and hot breath.
Water changes me.
I want to slide
and twist like a snake.
You tasted like
an orange sprinkled
with spice. I took
the tickle and spark
from the bumps
of your nipples and
counted them with
my tongue. When
I entered you,
you sprouted open
like a lily waiting
for my heat.
I drove you to
the purple threshold
between body and
soul. We were claimed
by the water and
sang it's falling song.
Later, in the window,
I read to you in French
from Cesaire, tying
language in ribbons.
We were caught
in envy's web
of silk and
blood.

THE TRIP TO MONTREAL, 1985

As the mountains
came into view just over
the border, you stuck
your head out the car window.
You let the air blow
through your short hair
and smiled that smile with
your teeth spelling happiness.
We drove into the city
and found a hotel nearly new,
next to a pavilion. The hotel
was gray and white.
In the restaurant, you wanted
me to speak French cause
I was fresh from Paris.
You didn't understand how
the English accent in French
is rough to the ear.
Only the French can turn
that exquisite slipping sound
that is the real thing,
a fancy slur. This was
French enough for you, and
you were thrilled to be here.
We was discoverers.
We was in *love.*

THE CAT WE NAMED KITTY, 1985

In Harlem he was raised
by a Chow Chow and never
figured out he was a cat.
At night up there on Hamilton Place,
he was small enough to sit
on the circle of your nipples.
We were in our little room
we made by putting up a sheet
for a curtain. We listened
as Gregory swooned us with
black women vocalists.
In the love songs, Kitty be
sliding off your titty like he was
on a sliding board trying to get
back to the top. You stole
his heart away from Gregory
in the time we lived in Harlem.
Somewhere inside you knew
this Kitty who played uptown smooth
would be your steady lover.
One time he almost died
with a swollen gall bladder.
You cried over this cat who could
charm you with his belly
breathing in time with your breasts
rising, rising, like he be
a black man for real.
Jive time cat don't even know
his real name is Soweto.

PRINCESS, 1986

My best friend Gene
was my best man. We waited
in Reverend Smallwood's study
for over an hour. At the house
y'all was fussing over hems
and laces and hair and makeup.
It was raining just a little bit,
not a bunch of sour tears,
but the kind that turn sweet.
Finally, the Lincoln Town Cars
turned the corner. I saw your foot
come out of the car, but I had
to wait until you came in the church.
Everybody was there,
your maids, my grooms, our families.
It was a wedding like I never
had before. It was a real wedding.
When you came in, I was
out of breath. You were
so stunning I wanted to kiss you
before we got to the ceremony.
I wanted to head for the honeymoon
waiting for us in Cape May
with the September summer.
I knew I had done the right thing
cause I cried those sweet tears.
If I live to be old, I will always
remember this day my princess
came to the altar in white,
her gown following her for a mile.
Amber, the flower girl,
spread petals for your feet.
Our wedding was a one day blossom
of an orchid garden with a path
winding to our ending, to the days
our marriage dried and fell away.

SUMMER IN SKOWHEGAN, 1990

I left you in a cabin
by the lake for the summer,
with the loon and the bugs.
After a month. I rented
a brown Volvo and drove
to visit you. At night,
the drive down the hill
to the cabins is treacherous
for the uninitiated. With night
runs for donuts in the painted bus,
you knew each tree and rock,
or at least you seemed
that happy. In the cafeteria
we could have endless vegetables
from Barbara, and you did.
It seemed you had forgotten
I was even there. You were in
a mind I had never seen, and
I was figuring how I could be rich
so that you could always do this.
I be thinking that way a lot.
I gave you the freedom
of space and time like I was rich,
and we thought that was marriage.
I was waiting for your body of work,
not realizing my kindness was
blocking the fury that you need.
You was standing by a tree
with your sun tan, smiling,
happy to be swimming in art,
thinking my love was free.

TELEPHONES, 1991

We came into Philly screaming,
me following you down 52nd street.
The seven hundred dollar phone bill
was too much like living large,
as if we was the Cosby's or some dream
like that, big time colored folk.
I screamed for a whole block.

When we got married, I got sick
and had to rest. You stayed,
so I believed I had to stay.
Commitment started adding up,
until we were thousands of dollars
into the heart's way of binding.
My soul wanted to leave, but
I could not hear. Then I tasted
my own flesh, hot and crisp,
my bones glowing red/yellow.

LITTLE GIRLS, 1993

The night I went to the play
and you waited on our steps,
I imagined you a little girl.
Somewhere in the fifties
on your steps on Spruce,
playing. It hurt me to see
you so innocent, as you can be
so innocent sometimes, and
here I was in the wilderness
of my own past, called out
of the wedding oath to slay
my dragon. My heart was broke,
broke and broken and overfilled
with itself. I cannot
make you see how one day
I awoke and had to follow
this need to break away.
I was in a cab coming home
late to the house you hated,
this brick assemblage built
seventy years ago. You hate it,
and I have since given it to you,
as it is the last material thing
I can give. I can't blame you.
I can only blame me for not striking
out against the way people come
to love me, despite my need to be
in the lonely room in East Baltimore
where I grew up. In a full house,
alone. I have to go back there
and find the *talisman* that has
made me a prisoner of love,
against the wishes of my dreams
at night, all gone in the bones.

MIZAN
...

MIDNIGHT DINNER, 1993

The boys played
a terrible trick on you,
snoring and acting the fool
while you did your monologue.
I took you to a restaurant
that was empty at first,
just a few folk who wander.
I played until I got your
birth date even though I knew
the year. I was just playing,
but I knew I would send
something to you every year.
I said the year you were born
like I didn't know, running a game
on you. You started rapid speech.
I knew your voice was trained.
You sat there and watched me
with your eyes moving real fast,
like a cat, without moving your head.
It was almost like you was afraid
of me. I wondered what you had seen
in the years you had lived,
what made you so suspicious.
I played, but I did not know how
to hang loose, to let a flirt be a flirt,
like the time I asked your zodiac sign
while we was playing in the *The Wok*.
You said "I am all signs."

FEVER, 1993

I ignored you
at the cast party cause
I was pure fire inside.
Every time I got near you
my skin sizzled like I was frying.
Still people realized flames
was jumping between us.
My mind was flying trip time
over wanting to be with you.
I drove you to the train station
in an all-white car, guarded
by the spirit of my Obatala,
surrounded by his white power.
Sade sang *No Ordinary Love,*
and each word made a mean rip
in my eyes. Tears wanted to fall
like little bad children. I tried
to think of something else.
I was someplace I didn't wanna be.
You walked away at the station
with your lovely legs and quick eyes.
I wanted to go with you.

THE VOICE FROM TRINIDAD, 1993

In the mornings,
I could hardly hold
a coffee cup. My hands
shook worse than some old man
with Parkinson's disease.
One day I could not stop
my right hand. It acted like
it was gonna come off my wrist.
I could only think about writing
if I was writing something
to you or for you. I was
stone gone. You had my nose
open wide enough to build a tunnel,
and I could only think of writing.
This first week after you left,
I cried quietly every afternoon.
I was losing weight, and a pain
started in my stomach. I was
in a world that would not let me be,
and you had called me "Love"
over the phone, using your voice.
I was dying. I was being born.

CHRISTMAS, 1993

I came back from Chicago
and discovered you loved me.
It was quite a shock.
You said it as I was walking
to the infamous door where earlier
in October I begged for a hug.
Now this love from this tiny voice
that can seem so in control on the phone.
"Love you," you said, and I almost
fell down, but I smiled and said
"You know I love you." I had learned
to know when you are in love
and what it means, after trying
to forget you in Chicago, near the lake.
I was beginning to think of friendship,
and now the scale was tipping again.
It is never a tranquil scale.
Still we did not kiss at the door.
You just stood there and watched me
all the way down the hallway.
I had learned how to leave quietly,
but you kept saying, "Call me. Call me."
I called you at New Year's and you said
"I think we are doing the right thing."
I still could not figure what was up with us.
Inside my heart there were two worlds.
My spirit struggled to stay sane.
My heart just kept on spilling over.
Father God, take this cup from my hand.

WHEN YOU SAY MY NAME, 1993

Sometimes you say it slow
and with a whine when I am
least prepared. When we drank
the punch at Mitali's at Christmas,
you got tipsy. Giggling,
you said, "I feel wonderful."
I smiled, but you whined
my name then, with your head
turned down, your hair flipping
just a little bit. I knew you wanted
something that called for words
you were afraid to speak.
You didn't want me to leave.
The winter was cold and tough.
Folk were scrambling to make a way
out of tests and temptations
from ice to running the hustle
to survive. New York is such a bitch
that way, teasing you with glitter.
You said my name again
and kicked your feet back and forth
like the little girl your father adored.
I knew that you could possibly
have wanted a number of things,
and I was certain of one
when you followed me to the door.
You sang that soft whining
that is your signal something inside
you is reaching out. I knew you
were not sure you wanted to be
held and kissed soft and hard.
I had to go, but I knew the key
in which you sang my name.

RED, 1994

In a letter I said I was giving
up acting like your lover.
Friendship was our limit.
We never kissed.
We never made love.
I bought a bunch of red shirts
because I loved red when
I was a little boy.
Plus I rented myself
a red Mercury and drove
to New York in a red streak
to see how you was taking
this most recent development.
You flirted so hard,
hollered back to see if I was looking,
"Did you bring your credit cards?"

Girl you betta watch yourself,
trying to tighten your hold on me.

HAL, 1994

Your answering machine died.
I hustled up to the Village
to comfort you. In your grief,
you remembered HAL
in his final decision-making.
Homeboy decided to edit
your friends, taking messages
only from the true hearts.
HAL knew where I was coming
from. That's why he gave up
his digital, electronic ghost.
We went to a coffee shop.
You wore a funny hat
as in memory of HAL.
A cat played under your feet
and kept pawing at the hat,
having felt your compadre's spirit.
We admired New York's skyline.
HAL left me big shoes to fill.
I spent two hundred dollars that day.
Many things step into the void
that Death leaves behind.

Walking to the subway stairs,
I bought you three bunches of lilacs.
This bright yellow shoots from
the earth where your father asked you
to place him, which you dutifully did.
Watching me go down undergound,
you whispered a crackled goodbye.

EPIPHANY, 1994

All the changes made me feel
like I was throwing myself
against your heart. It is
a city of crystal and gold.
I got you to crack the door,
but you only peeped out at me
like the little colored girls
in my elementary school.
Maybe that's where you sent me,
back home to the beginning.
Maybe you took away my excuses.
I dreamed of us making love,
and you peeped from your heart.
I knew then you needed me,
but all that slamming up against
this city of crystal and gold
made me slide down and feel foolish.
I rubbed all my clothes off
as I slid down the wall to the water
cause you sure nough live in the sea.
I was all the way naked there,
and the fish that are your little powers
stared at me, but I did not drown.
One day I just turned in a circle
on the water and looked at the walls.
I looked and looked until something
appeared to me from the hardness.
I saw myself in a king's raiments
holding myself in my hands.

FRIENDSHIP, 1994

"Companion friends love each other."
—Laurence Thomas

I stayed away
for two months, caught up
in myself, wondering
if we were friends. The day
I came back Sango was
making thunder over us.
I could see myself
in things I mailed to you.
We walked to *Mitali's.*
I followed, afraid
of my anger and yours.
In the rain, stepping sideways,
we went for another Indian lunch.
I was beginning to see
my love was my first love
rising again from its grave.
With a doggy bag, we walked
to Sixth Avenue, went over reviews
of *Alma's Rainbow*, your film.
We parted, you with the food,
your feet in black sneakers.
At Penn Station I got lost in
the chatter of commuters.
I grabbed my New York Post
for the gossip, bought a bottle
of water. It wasn't my grief,
my offering of gifts to you, *Osun,*
to set your soul aflame. No,
my loneliness was all over me,
a new temple over this body,
my own demons. Train stations
are where I feel the exchange
of life's weight, spirit to spirit.
Time has a gift that is not time.

NOTES: 1. Bessie is my mother, born Elsie Lee Davis on December 5, 1929 in Valentines, Virginia to Ashton Davis and Gracie (Goode) Davis. In 1950 in Baltimore she married my father, Otis Ruffin Weaver and gave birth to five children. In chronological order, we are Afaa Michael Schan, Marva Jean, Michele Dorsette, Marlene Ruth, and Mark Joseph. Marlene's children are Alya Amani and Sean Ruffin McNeill.

2. Eleanora is my first wife, born Eleanora Maddox. In 1970 we were married when I was nineteen and she was eighteen. We had two sons, Michael Jr., who died in his sleep at ten months, and Kala Oboi who is alive and healthy. Kala was born in 1973, and we gave him his West/Central African name, Kala Oboi.

3. Ronetta is my second wife, born Ronetta Irene Barbee. In 1978 we were married when I was twenty-six and she was twenty-five. We had no children.

4. Aissatou is Aissatou Mijiza, my third wife, born Gwendolyn Elizabeth Warr. In 1986 we were married when I was thirty-four and she was thirty-two. We had no children.

5. Mizan is Mizan Kirby Nunes, the stage and film actress. A Trinidadian, she lives in New York. In the spring of 1993, we met in Philadelphia. We are companion friends.

Afaa M. Weaver, formerly known as Michael S. Weaver, is a poet and playwright. A veteran of fifteen years (1970-1985) as a blue collar worker in factories in his native Baltimore, he became a published poet, fiction writer, and journalist. He received an NEA fellowship for poetry while working in the factories, where he was a ware-houseman in the last ten years of his blue collar worker life which he began in the steel mills. In 1985 he was accepted in the Creative Writing program at Brown University, where he received his M.F.A. degree. *Talisman* is his sixth published collection of poetry. His previous collection was *Timber & Prayer*, from University of Pittsburgh Press. His new play is *Candy Lips & Hallelujah*. His play *Elvira and the Lost Prince* was one of the first recipients of the Playwrights Discovery/Development Initiative (PDI) Award in Chicago at ETA Creative Arts Foundation. He is now a panel member of PDI, and he is a member of the inaugural faculty of Cave Canem, the first workshop retreat for African-American poets. He is the editor of *Obsidian II*, the review of Black Literature located at North Carolina State University in Raleigh. In the spring of 1997, he served as the sixteenth Poet in Residence at Bucknell University.

Afaa M. Weaver teaches at Rutgers and Simmons College.